BIRDS
of
PASSAGE

COLLECTION OF POEMS

Kunwar Siddharth

INDIA · SINGAPORE · MALAYSIA

Notion Press

Old No. 38, New No. 6
McNichols Road, Chetpet
Chennai - 600 031

Re-published by Notion Press 2018
Copyright © Kunwar Siddharth 2018
All Rights Reserved.

ISBN
Hardcase Indian 978-1-64249-048-0
Paperback Indian 978-1-64892-994-6
Paperback International 978-1-64899-669-6

Contents

Dear Carmela,

I wish you all the happiness and joy in life.

- Kunwar

Dedicated to

My family, friends, and teachers.

पोथी पढ़ि पढ़ि जग मुआ, पंडित भया न कोय ।
ढाई आखर प्रेम का, पढ़े सो पंडित होय ।।

Reading millions of Books and Scriptures
Everyone died, none became wise.

Whoever reads the words of love,
He is the wisest of the wise.

– **Kabir**

The Beginning

At the beginning of the journey, there was an infinite void.

What are these sun, stars, and earth?

Why are these days and nights?

How does a bird fly?

Where does this river flow?

Who am I?

At the beginning of the journey,

There was an incomprehensible dream.

The path of life is curious and long.

The beauty and stories of the world lie

Hidden in the mountains of the unknown.

The pearls of truth lie deep in the ocean

Of knowledge and inquiries.

At the beginning of the journey, perfume

And joy blossom in the serenity of heart.

The wings of freedom are unstretched

For their completion.

The seeds of love and peace remain

To be scattered in the soil of each day.

The instrument of music is unrehearsed

For the songs of the feast.

At the beginning of the journey, death is beyond.

And the grip of fear is weak and subtle.

Now, all the ropes of safety and care

Must be unmoored from the harbour of the homeland.

O' "The Captain of Thy Ship,"

"The Uninitiated Sailor."

Muster all your strength.

And now, you must sail in this great

Sea of the "adventure of life."

Signposts

Like in the far countryside
Some cluster of lamps outside people homes
Would ignite hopes and aspirations
Of a wayfarer passing by.
Let some stars shining brightly in the sky
And sending their light from infinity,
Would be enough to raise your heart.
And give you strength and light
On your long journey ahead.

Like a flower which lives in a pond.
Away from the town,
Away from the sight of the common.
But there it grows day and night.
Blossoms and gives its fragrance to the surroundings.
Let you find solace,
A quiet space in your daily endeavour.
Where you can be still, ponder, grow day and night
And spread your essence all around you.

Like in the long dreary path of a desert.

In silent, keen and pervading heat,

The mere sound of birds or their fleeting appearance

Are some helpful guide to find a nearby oasis.

Let some words here, and the voice of yours,

Which will soon vanish

Be subtle hints to some hidden treasure within you.

Brimfull

The music in our life,

Songs which are not sung, yet stay at our brim.

One moment with you my mother nature,

One moment with you my beloved friends,

And I ever flow like a new river.

A butterfly quest for serenity,

The great ocean surrenders to the soil of the shore,

An unyielding mountain and your compassionate eye

Break all impediments around us,

And our heart plunge in jubilations.

In these meetings,

At such reinvigorating moments,

We would never hold on to ourselves.

We would cry out all our miseries.

We would dance, sing and free every emotion

Held deep in our hearts.

Friends,

Do not stop me today.

And let this ecstasy go on

Until this vessel is all empty.

However, time passes soon enough.

All our tedious days will come again and again

And fill every hour with the gloomy cloud of discontent.

Our shoulder goes down by the duties

And burdens of the world.

"Is there any rule here as such?"

"Who cares what someone will say to me?"

"Who will punish me for what?"

Instant this impatient heart becomes unrest and saturated,

I leave everything and run to this paradise,

Which is always present and lives so near to me.

Away from Aviary

I have dreams to go far and far in the sky
To see what lies beyond the horizon of my vision.
I have dreams to search all the corners of this home
For any lost desire of my heart.

I have dreams to feel the strength of different soil
And let me know the firmness of my leg.
I have dreams to chase these clouds,
To know wherever they go
And let me see their formation and how they rain.

I have dreams to go back, to the earliest,
When everything started, such that I would know
What led everything here.
I have dreams to go on the moon,
To stay there for a while
And leave all delusions of belonging only to earth.

My home is large and plentiful,

However, my stay is temporary.

And reaching over the edge of all known

Horizons in this life,

I have dreams to surpass what was even unsurpassable.

Alchemy of Wind

A gust of wind has come from far beyond,

Held in it, stories and fragrance of the unknown.

The rustling of leaves, the swinging of branches of trees

Are gestures of ecstasy float in common.

Sitting by the bank of a river,

I found myself slowly drawn in this sunken pleasure.

A little time that I squandered in

Drinking from this floating barrel,

From this mystic wind,

Mind got absent from the world

And eyes drawn to wishful sleep.

In this moment of oblivion

"What special message has been whispered in our heart?"

What has been done to us to live and die in a moment?

Which sanctify liquid could ever have such effect?

With flashes of light into the mind comes
The new awakening.
The enlightened heart sees the world
With new vision and delight.

Elixir of life is no longer a secret quest,
What was ever sought only through
Gleaming and strayed eyes.
To sit and let yourself be drawn towards oneself
And lost in a moment, is the true way of seeking.

Join the Children Play

Do not disturb us today,

We are busy here; we are playing our daily games.

We are collecting many toys and often

Snatch it from our peers,

Whichever we like.

We are playing all day with these

Costly toys without any rest.

However, when we get bored, we throw them,

Toss them up and down, until they completely break,

And we even laugh and cheer doing so.

Do not make us bother to take home so early.

We are singing and dancing for unknown reasons.

We are making loud noises without any chorus.

We are singing without any words.

We are jumping in the air,

Shaking our legs without any rhythm.

Borne in the joy of play, we are running in every direction

And we don't know where we are going.

Do not lure us for any precious gift.

Our greatest treasure lies in this play,

Full of other children.

In our friendship, we are holding each other hands

And hugging them all, full of grace.

Without any prejudice.

We are waving our hands to all wayfarers

Without bothering for any return.

Do not scare or scold us such that

Our cloth may get tattered or dirty.

We are playing in the dust and on the

Grass as our sleeping bed.

We are playing with all other animals as our own being.

We are chasing dogs and cats, and they chase us too.

We are making birds fly, and they perch

On our shoulders and play with us.

Please forgive all our mistakes as

We are playing without any rules,

Without any win or loss.

Do not get bound forever in your daily work,

Or to any otherworldly games.

If you desire to be children again and eager to join.

Then free yourself from yourself,

And come play with us.

Songs of Lovebirds

You smile from your busy work,

Passing subtle hints to let me come near you.

But your piercing eyes would send me away for no reason.

I clutch your hands to pull you in my arms.

You resist and struggle to go away.

But your heavy breath and loud beating

Heart always want to be held.

Words and gestures have no meaning in our life.

Our love is ignorant of what things

Said or what understood.

Two ecstatic sparrows,

Heavily drunk with some elixir of life,

Chase one another in our verandah.

They flap their wings, go here and there and

Would play among them all day.

They sing and speak whatever means to them.

Their songs and jubilations would fill our silent days here.

In those branching moments,

When we had given ourselves in each other arms

And completely drowned in the fragrance of our breath,

My peaceful heart would listen and remember those songs

That you practice and murmur only to yourself.

When I am not here,

Gone very far from you,

In some strange or dreadful places.

When there is no sleep in the night,

Then some sweet memories

Of our delightful useless struggle

Would fill my loneliness with much fleeting joy.

Roots of A Tree

Embed Yourself.
Get your grip tighten firmly now.

Slowly and steadily,
Seeking the kernel of your own heart

Unseen to the whole world,
Yet working day and night.

Digging deeper and deeper,
Within yourself and way around.

Quietly searching for,
Your true nourishment.

The Lover's Nest

A bird of passage my life has wandered far and wide.
This wearisome journey has gone to countries unknown
And sought for things of no worth.

After such a long and relentless quest,
This lost bird has found its nest within your eyes.
This torn-apart heart from in-numerous rejections
Is sewn by your generous and compassionate gazes.

In this beautiful sanctuary,
We get peace and comfort ever desired.
Your sober and sympathetic words give joy and freedom
To all our fervent emotions
And these poems come out of nowhere.

My beloved friend,
Please keep this door of love ever open to us.
When our wings will be tired
From the long tumultuous struggle of laborious life.
When this head would bow down,
And the sunset is near.

With hopes to find shelter and rest.

With hopes to rediscover our real self.

We would only seek to these dark eyes,

Which are our true home.

Flowering

With peaceful whispers in the morning,
First rays of light and the whole universe
Conjured up its strength
And plea to the lotus-
The daybreak is near now
And night is gone far ahead.
Do not linger more in your sleep.
Open your petals,
And let this life unfold.

The fragrance of you may spread
Around and bring joy in the heart.
Your colour may brighten the whole pond
And bring life to the picture.
The sky is blue and clear without any trace of clouds.
Spring of youth may pass too soon,
And your colour might fade.
Do not delay.
Open your petals,
And let this beauty unfold.

Grass and hedges are waiting patiently to be delighted.

Your other friends in the pond

Are waiting for you to bloom.

The fresh wind of the morning may pass too soon.

Everyone here is perplexed and eagerly enquires-

What special message you hide in your heart.

Do not fear.

Open your petals,

And let this mystery unfold.

Water and ground beneath are there to hold you tight.

The sky waits to kiss you from drops of morning mist.

Birds are ready with their greeting songs.

The whole world is queued and waits only for you.

Greet them all and let all the joy and

Beauty of life flow through you.

Do not shy.

Open your petals,

And let this story unfold.

I

I am the miracle of light;
Whose mere presence is a great epoch
In the existence of the whole universe.
I am the one, part of the whole and whole itself.
I am a small wave in the ocean and the ocean itself.

I am the bird that is traveling to the unknown and beyond
In this magnificent sky of life.
I am the mud whose shape is ever-changing,
Moulding and becoming new again and again.

I am the seeker of my goal and the goal itself.
I am the love of my beloved and beloved himself.
I am the presence and consciousness of the presence
Beyond the sense of time and form.

Late Monsoon

The sky waits.

The land waits.

Wait every being around.

Every impatient heart speaks loud and loud.

Come monsoon,

Come early this year,

And bring heavy rain from far

Our days are running and going to "where is water"

And "where-is shade."

Nights are still and keen without any wind.

In-home children wait.

In the forest Peacock wait.

Come monsoon,

To free us all from the clutch of this pervasive heat

And bring heavy rain from far.

This year summer was ever cruel to us.

It's already too late for us.

All dry crops in field wait.

Withered leaves on trees and droop flowers wait.

Day and night, they all look in the sky and sing.

Come monsoon.

Do not delay.

Come early in June.

Come with all lightning and thunder,

And bring heavy rain from far.

Boundless Identity

Not in the name.

Nor in any specific place.

We do not belong to any of these.

And our identity is boundless.

The fetter of life is life itself.

Not in some principle.

Nor in any subject of competence.

We do not belong to any of these.

Of infinite lives that live here,

We are one of them.

And our identity is boundless.

The fetter of life is life itself.

Your Stubborn Anklets

Don't pull us from your smile towards yourself,

We have much work to do.

Today, we will go to some other town,

And your bangles start to jingle loudly.

We promise to come back soon,

But your eyes are not talking to us.

As we are leaving home and going,

Your anklets run hurriedly and stop us on the door.

Don't stand at the doorway when we are long gone,

As we have a long way to go.

Orchestra

Come today.
Come all neighbours.
To listen what musician plays
And to know what his instrument is.

A group of pigeons would come and go to
Whatever pull them here.
Some friends who live nearby yet far apart.
Grace has come from such attention
And our heart is puffed up and raised.
All gather and sit patiently around.
The dubious murmur in people has entangled
And spread hidden mystery in the air.

With a simple tune,
And with a simple song,
A piece of sober music begins to play.
Silence breaks and smiles rippled through everywhere.

When musician swings his bow, our head swing, leg swing

And our heart jumps in the air.

Like a good captain, musician sailed the ship through

Many whizzes and turn,

And everyone borne deep in the ocean of joy.

Like a sprinkle of soft rain,

Delight wet us all and fall everywhere.

Please play some more songs,

There come many humble requests

From people back in the chair.

All-day this music goes on,

All-day rhythm up and down,

All-day claps around

And all day just one more new desire.

When evening comes,

The light fades,

The music fades.

Nattering many songs in our hearts,

We slowly retreat to our homes.

In the night, in our deep sleep,

Someone from elsewhere would pull some strings

And songs start to play in our dream.

She who takes a deep sigh and silent melody

Run in our longing.

This, that is our great heart, seeks music everywhere.

"The Rhythm," "where is his rhythm?"

He goes and wanders far for music.

He stops not even in a dream,

Nor in any other moment of life.

From your slumber,

And from all weariness.

Come again,

Come all friends.

To make your ear true and listen-

Deep sorrow and deadly cry in thunder

And lightning within the clouds.

The drizzle of rain, which stirs many strings

Of the heart and plays love songs.

The jubilant and clamorous waves,

Which bring out all the ecstasy hidden deep in the ocean.

The joy of life, mirthful delight in the chirping of birds.

And this continuous soft background

Music that is played by air

Through the rustling of leaves.

Let us stay for a while and do not move along,

And listen to this great music that is always played

And surrounds us everywhere.

Fettered

This dry desert and no voice near,

This nothing inside me.

A lot of water here, everywhere,

But this unquenched thirst always resides in me.

You have made me ambiguous,

When you went so far from me.

In meeting with friends and people,

If I talk, I talk to no one.

Whenever I look in the mirror,

I don't see my face.

I disappear and cannot be seen.

You have taken myself from me,

When you went so far from me.

I wander and roam about,

Singing songs of love and longing.

Friends do not come near; in fear, it would be a pity.

Sages console with some wise words,

And then they move along.

You have taken all my friendship.

When you went so far from me.

Waves of your joyful memories strike daily

On the shore of this ocean heart.

I would cry, and tears would spread all around me.

I am forever caged in this abiding pain of your love.

You have taken my freedom,

When you went so far from me.

Resurrection

Sprouting seeds from the soil.

Lotus opening its petals.

Sun rising behind.

Voice of the Cuckoo from the distant trees.

The sudden rush of blood in our limbs.

Listlessly, we move towards the light.

The revival of new in the old.

Leaving behind our shadow on the bed of time.

The stories of love and despair.

The unquenched thirst of in-numerous desires.

In the barren soil of recurrent days.

There is an incessant shower of sunshine.

Rise and bloom of flowers every day.

Lamp of The Dark Night

যদি আলো না ধরে, ওরে ও অভাগা, যদি ঝড়-বাদলে আঁধার রাতে দুয়ার দেয় ঘরে তবে বজ্রানলে আপন বুকের পাঁজর জ্বালিয়ে নিয়ে একলা জ্বলোরে ।।

If the dark night brings a storm at the door –

Then let the lightning ignite the light in you alone to shine on the path

If no-one heeds your call - then walk alone.

– **Ekla Chalo Re, Rabindranath Tagore**

You, that have come so far.

You, that dream to go so far.

Your journey is long ahead,

Whom do you trust so much?

Your journey is scary,

Who is your best friend?

Deep down this road,

Through every turn and in every way,

Many blind processions would march along beside you.

Looking at you earnestly,

With the hope that you may join them.

Beguiling you with their ardent and fiery summons.

Their drums and clamour always

Hovering above your head.

Are you afraid then and eager to go?

Should you not hold yourself and enquire-

Where they are heading?

From where did they come?

If you do not search for truth from yourself,

Then you may drift towards what is most popular.

If you do not see from yourself,

A popular vision may drift towards you.

Be that as it may-

Think who is so resourceful that

Guided you in every pathway till here.

And who makes to see ahead before any venture you took.

Be that as it may-

What if in those dark nights, in that windy storm

When the light of all truth is blown away.

When your vision is fogged by the

Untruth world present before you.

And what if fear creep into your legs,
And the whole world waits to see
That you might give up and fall in their trap.
In their deception of coercion.

Listen to a truthful voice somewhere deep in your heart
May hold you back and assert-

Might of all the might, "to say no," "to disagree,"
"To find your own way" and
"To light your own lamp" to go ahead.

Anhhilation

People from my village have come in their sympathy.
They called this madness,
Pity me and sit beside in consolation.
The teaching of the wise will surrounds me
But this sobbing never stop.
Being ineffective they go away.

This heartfelt cry, this painful longing for you
Has pushed me in the impenetrable darkness.
Tears do not stop; the body becomes weak and fragile
With little strength to uphold.
Stories of our love and separation
Are in every home today.
But no one can ever fathom this pain.

How to tell the world that,
What everything one has can be lost in a moment
And neither did I know what was truly lost.
But a huge vacancy everywhere.
Sky of emptiness covers me wherever I go.

The dark clouds with thunder and lightning
Always hover over my heart.

But a few days later,
A cool breeze comes over and passes through.
Heavy sleep has taken hold on me in its lap.
A peaceful sleep in this deathly abyss.

Mirage of Light

Trumpet of the world market

A call for gullible.

Light chasing the shadow.

Blinded by immediate vision.

Folded in limits of pace.

Deranged.

Stranger in Homeland

Many a fleeting moment pass by sitting
At the shore of the ocean
And looking far beyond the horizon.
Chilling wind draws oneself inward.
Waves come and go, washing the feet
And taking some sand with it.
Ground moves beneath and detachment
Comes with a pang in the heart.
Echoes of waves knock some uninhabited room inside.

In my deep urges, I wait for a boat to come
From eternity and take me there.
Lightning and thunder in some far away cloud.
Longing for a new home with a vision of
Strange people flashes over eyes
And these unknown feelings have made
Me a stranger from my homeland.

After years of waiting, a boat has come now,
And I must prepare for my journey.
At the time of departure, people of my village
Have come to bid me

And brought food and supply for the sail.

Their love binds my legs,

But my boat is already unmoored.

Mystery and wonder of meeting with new people took

Hold on me throughout my journey.

The boat of life is anchored to a new destination.

On reaching a new land mist forms in the eyes.

An elation, joy, and mirth of tired

Waves reaching to the shore.

Coming to a new place is to be born again.

Everything looks fresh and new to the eyes,

Even the twinkling of the stars.

The course of life goes through many such journeys

And to the various places until a boat

Of death would come at last.

Then this wandering,

This temporary stay at many places would

Become some old memories

That too I can't take with me.

Heart wonders!

Where do I truly belong?

Where is the permanent stay?

I myself don't know.

Either I belong to everywhere or nowhere.

Death of New Everyday

Today, when the morning is pure and fresh as ever.
When the dewdrops of mist are scintillating
Every ray of light
And birds are echoing their mirthful songs of the feast
In the thickest of the forest.

Today, when flowers are opening their buds of love to
Spread fragrance and youth in the air.
When children and ducks in the pond are plundering
All the joy from this abundance
And dancing for no reason.

Today, when the vast immensity of stillness
Of the night can be grasped
By the mere chirping of crickets.
When all the life brim over with unknown pleasure
And is tuned to the music of eternal,
My mused heart is held captive in some
Life's well-trodden paths.

It is in this heart that the songs of old are all sunk,

And it is the death of new every day.

The eyes of the heart are closed and strayed

Far in some strange loneliness

When beauty and life are unfolding.

See from Above

Declare yourself as small as any particle.

Of sort nothing.

Like dust in the air.

Such that no words or shame can break you more.

There lies a place beyond language and knowing,

Where every other being lives.

Go at such high altitude,

Within yourself.

Such that no flattery or praise

May ever reach you there.

Declare yourself as light as feathers,

And do not bother to uplift the burden

Of ages over your shoulder.

A bird escapes the aviary and learns

Deliverance by wings of struggle.

Break all your bonds by wings of detachment.

And go above everything,

To see everything.

We are Lazy, We are Slow

Life goes on here, everywhere,
We don't bother.
We are sleeping deeply in our bed,
Fully absorbed in our dreams.
No quest, nothing, whatsoever.

In the early morning, some birds would alarm us
By their chirping and singing
But their friendly efforts never wake us.
Our body is lazy enough to get up early
And open doors and windows to let the sunshine come.
Nothing goes out; nothing comes in.

Suddenly, a wanderer bee would enter from nowhere.
Her hovering and humming disturb our peace,
But we did not mind her presence.
Let her sit where she wants to sit
Or share our food with us.
We like the presence of such lovely
Guests in our empty rooms.

Around our home a herd of cattle passes through,

Chewing their food slowly and continuously,

Stewing saliva from their mouth wherever they go.

Sounds of their bells that hang around their necks

Do not stir any rhythm in us.

Day and night, we don't ponder too much on anything.

We pass every deep thought that comes to us.

"Who cares?"

We are very idle to think deeply.

We are laughing loudly at every meaningless

Joke that comes to us.

We don't wait or strain our head for

Creating the wiser one.

We are not swayed by any famous stories

Happening around the world.

What "someone said something" or

"Who did what to whom."

We are deeply sad for many days by the death of a moth

In his love for light near our lamp.

We don't study poetry or recite any great

Quote to inspire ourselves.

Our heart is raised to the sky, when,

For any trivial job well done,

Any trivial thought well said,

Our friends pat us from behind

With their exclamatory or jumble words like-

"Aahaaaaaa! Bhai Waah! Kya Baat Hai! Bahut Bandhiyan!"

We are silent for hours and hours,

No gesture, speaking nothing.

Giving ample time to let our heart speaks his desire.

Let all joy and sorrow come out from him

With no obstruction from our minds.

Our days are lazy enough to reach the night

And nights are always lost in counting stars.

We don't go to the zoo,

Forest or any other wild places for recreation.

The movement of the lizard on our

Wall and hunt for his food

Create great awe and adventure in us.

How galaxy and star move around in the universe,

We never care.

We are struck and amaze by the movement

Of the fan above our head.

We don't compete with this world for any great pride,

Honour or high morals.

And certainly, we are not seeking intelligence

As any great virtue in us.

We are living cordially with all virtue we know.

We do not worry if we lack behind in the queue

Or may miss bus or train.

Many will come for us.

We are going and stopping at our own pace.

Let this world go so fast with such

Haste to wherever it is going.

But we are here.

Happily absorbed in ourselves,

With what is easy and what is near.

Unmoved by any pull or force of the world.

Summoning

Come my friend and find me in this

Infinite maze of time and place.

Come from your difficult journey and keep

Your hands on my chest

And stop this everlasting cry for you.

This unceasing pain and emptiness that

Chained me wherever I go.

Echo of my own voice that speaks so loudly in my ear.

Come to silence them all.

A song that we both started to sing together,

A hand that is half held.

Come my friend to finish our song

And complete our meeting.

Cosmic Gifts

When you find mud is all around you,

Pulling you further and deeper.

If all grace has been lost and you are going only down,

Deeper and deeper.

To pull you up above and get you to some high ground.

Take your head up.

Take your spirit up,

And look at the stars.

When emptiness surrounds you

And your heart is held captive in some deep sorrow.

If sad and gloomy eyes see darkness everywhere

And there is no one beside to lighten you up.

At your service patiently waiting for many ages.

Sending their love and light from such

Far and expecting that-

Only for one moment you may see nowhere,

And only look at the stars.

When everything is lost that took years to build

And destruction is everywhere.

If you can't see any horizon beyond

Dark and roaring clouds,

Let you wait for a wind of love to come from far

And then there will be a shower of care and friendship.

Let you wait for a wind of strength to build around

To blow every cloud of doubt,

And then there will be raining light

From scintillating stars.

Come hither every day.

Come into open ground.

To dance and sing on the edges of these diamond rays.

To wet in this raining love.

Look at the sky,

And look at the stars.

Escaped

For many years this world has forged and
Strengthened solid bars around me
To hold me captive within myself.
Fear has chained my legs and let me not
Move one step forward.

Shame has guarded my way around so keenly.
It has watched every move taken,
Every gesture made, words said or said not
With absolute precision.
Pride and dignity have made a wall so high to jump above.
I tried my way beyond, pushed myself
Harder with all force but failed.

Around here, mistakenly,
They have left open a small window
To let air and sunshine could come
Through in this dungeon.

For long did I waited for you.

For long did I called your name within.

And for my luck, you heard me.

Soon, by following the echo of my voice,

And by eluding all gatekeepers,

You came and saw me,

And I escaped.

Glitter of the Evening Cloud

The story of a new night begins with the melting of sun
And with its fading light.
Our daily work is over.
A gentle breeze from nearby lake hurriedly comes
And fills the dry air with the fragrance of many flowers.
The gloomy shadows become bigger and die.

We retreat to our homes with weakening
Urges and tired limbs.
The day closes for today and birds sing no more.
At this annihilating moment when the
Beauty of the day is at its peak,
Time slows.
Clouds glitter at their edge and spread gold everywhere.

We arrive at our homes, in friends, and families.
Soft smiles pervade everyone's face
And our heart is filled with no rush.

Fill your Heart with Sky

Let all the years come through and various
Season of life pass aside.
Hereafter, fill your heart only with the sky.
Who is so free and more powerful?

The tumultuous and unrestful days
Of summer would come
And fill our days and night with the warm air of hope.
On the dawn of spring,
Our pain leaves by seeing the approaching heavy clouds.
The heart rejoices and loses itself
And pouring of rain begins which wet us in tears of joy.

When there is deep sadness lingered around,
Long silence hovers in the air
And it creates a storm with the lightning
Of many jolt and thunder of deep cries.
These are the dangerous moment that can
Destroy everything you have.
Hold on to yourself for now.

Never loses your faith.

The mighty storm will last only for a few moments.

Peace will come soon in our hearts and then

There would be a clearer sky.

On calm and lazy months,

When idleness freezes our youth at the house

Of some old winter dead habits.

Soon, sunny days of autumn arrive knocking

Our door and windows.

Warm sunshine that comes with it melts

All our frozen thoughts.

A new leaf of many creative ways will start

To appear in a bright and colourful sky.

Let all these seasons pass through and years

Of life come again and again.

Hereafter, fill your heart only with the sky.

Which is endless and shall ever remain unyielding.

Connoisseur

It is one trick.

Not the hard one.

But the simplest one.

Every artist in the world practicing

Their simple and basic notes.

Day and night,

And for many years.

With some vigour,

With some joy in their hearts,

All are listening and refining to what is simple and sober.

Practicing again and again.

Million times over.

Singers are rhyming the 'taal,' musician are playing

Basic notes with their instrument again and again.

They are practicing and listening to simple notes

With the depth of attention.

Removing any small noise from it

And day by day they are becoming a wise connoisseur.

Washers are washing clothes more clearly day by day.

How easily and with such agility,

They wash so many clothes.

No hidden trick behind.

But the simplest one.

Beating the clothes many times over on stone.

Accuracy comes to him through much practice.

Tillers are tilling the road within some handful of strokes.

Being aware of how much strength should be

Applied to hard and soft soil.

Precision comes to him through experiences.

How chefs are making special food within some minutes

And for many people.

Day to day they discard what is not tasty or odourless.

But their preference is always of simple test

Over any other taste.

It became delicious or smells great by the

Addition of extra flavour of spice

On clean and simple foods.

Sages meditate silence and peace for many years

And they are tuned to the greatest of all music.

Every wise thing said to them will be discarded,

If it is not tuned to their heart if it is not peaceful.

All our life, inadvertently, we too practice

Simple notes day and night.

From virtue of our presence,

We are looking at this beautiful world,

Filled with various kind and joyful life in it.

We are seeing the sun in the day,

Star and moon in the night.

We are looking into endless sky,

Ocean and to high mountains.

From all this scenery, our sight and our mind are tuned.

The songs of birds around us,

Rain pouring and flowing of the river.

All these are resonating in our heart again and again,

And tuning us forever to the music of the world.

We are sleeping at night and being silent for many hours.

"Our likes and dislikes".

Every action, every choice made is an act of refinement.

The movement towards what is peaceful

And musical to our hearts.

Movement from haste to peace and comfort.

Day and night, and through all years of life

We are making our heart tuned to whatever we truly love,

Whatever we truly see as beautiful.

Every day, all are playing their simple and basic notes.

Day and night, and for many years.

With some vigour,

With some joy in the heart,

Every artist is listening and refining their taste.

Practicing their art, again and again,

A million times over.

And sometimes,

Great music comes from deep within our hearts.

What is Left of Me is this Love

Along Your Way

Be that as it may brother.

Take this whole world for naught.

Care not what it says or means.

With humble self and peace on the forehead.

You must move along your way.

The day-and-night world buzz around with its hustle

And many unknown races.

Showing and telling about its own

Extraordinary splendour.

Belittling you.

Shrinking your high aspirations.

Be that as it may brother.

Take all their grandeur for naught.

With a great heart and a magnificent soul.

You must move along your way.

In this big market of hallucination,

Beautifully packed merchandise

And wine of pleasure with varying flavours

Are brought daily before you.

Bargaining your taste and desire.

Be that as it may brother.

Take all their rich and rare pleasure for naught.

With sobriety and joy that spread abundantly

In your conscious and peaceful moments.

You must move along your way.

From the depth of your sleep and awakened moments.

The love of your life and the place of your dreams,

Summoning your name through

Many hardships of struggle.

Questioning your strength.

Challenging your patience.

Be that as it may brother.

Take your doubts for naught.

With any broken strength and lost faith.

You must move along your way.

Into the sky of limitless future.

Into the treasure and adventure of finding and losing.

Tough and alone it might be my brother.

With the perfume of grace around you.

You must move along your way.

The Desire to Stay

I have my earnest wish to tell you today

When you will meet me at our love tryst.

I do not want that our meeting should depart.

From evening and through all the night.

Like a sleep that covers a tired soul,

Like a moth near a lamp.

In your company

And in your arms,

I have the desire to stay

Let there be many birds sing around in the park.

Let the beauty and fragrance of flowers

Blossom in this tranquil wind.

Or someone might play the flute near us.

We would not pay any heed to them.

In this grey moonlight.

Like a freshness of the morning.

Like a simple rhythm that stays on our lips

Long after being heard.

In your eyes

And on your lips,

I have the desire to stay.

We walk and a love discourse moves through us.

Our heart plays along and chases each other

Like ripples of water over the river.

Glorious sky shows his gladness for these meetings

Through the twinkling of stars.

In the presence of many legends around us,

In their care.

Like a softness that stays in morning flowers.

Like a light that stays in the sun.

In your heart

And in your life,

I have the desire to stay.

The Transient Portal

Like two stray birds, we are lost.

Chasing and stretching our arms for thirst unknown.

Hugging and kissing gently on each other cheeks.

Seeking our roots in these branching moments.

These are the crevasses through

Which light and music enter.

Not the word we spoke but silences between them.

Not that we looked at each other all night

But through fleeting gazes.

The Birds of Passage

Every morning some stranger birds would wake me,

Stir me from dreamy sleep.

They are always punctual as a clock

And don't mind the harsh weather.

I wonder if I could ever plea

With them not to come so early,

Let me sleep for some more hours, disturb me not.

Let me go to my busy dreams

And complete my precious sleep.

Sometimes I try to shoo them,

Make them go away but felt guilty whenever I do so.

If I can decipher, I want to know-

What is their message for me?

What is their song about?

Are they the ones who came yesterday?

Or today some other birds from elsewhere?

They stay beside our home,

On rooftops, making this silent

And joyless world listens to their continuous chirping.

A fakir migrates to different cities, to many strange places,
Singing some mystical songs that no one understands.
What's their business in this passage of the world?
Only these birds would know.

Our enigmatic heart expresses our true desire.
It makes us love strangers
And humbly acknowledge any foreign land as its home.
Inadvertently, how we learned this art of living?
Only these birds would know.

My Heart Seeks Your Love

Seeker of all seekers, our heart,

Have brought us to this love tryst.

To plea with you.

To get from you what can never be

Found in the whole universe.

And that, only you can give us.

Do not make us return

Or shame us with your wise words.

As a big ocean, you always surround us.

And a thirsty fish of my heart asks,

To give us your love.

On our way here,

Many storms we faced,

But waves were not large enough to drown us.

Many dreadful places we passed through,

But the path was not dangerous enough to shake our faith.

The shroud of dust, the shroud of poverty

Covers us all through the way.

Take these hands and hold it firmly.

Take us away from this whole world,

To cover us in the shroud of your care and friendship.

And give us your love.

Day-and-night pass at such a brisk pace here.

These times will pass too.

Soon death will come to us,

And this life will be only some fleeting memories.

Make this endless.

Free us from the fetter of life and death.

And give us your love.

The Jewels of Light

This is what our bond here is.

The sun comes every morning,

Knocking on our door of eyes,

Spreading its golden light to every dark corner.

The world is ecstatic in joy.

The subtle celebration is all around.

Every being walks on earth with their head held high.

From this enormous treasure,

Our life is rich and prosperous.

When sun bids farewell at dusk,

Then our course retreat.

The tired body searches shelter to hide and rest.

But for our delight stars and moon come in the sky

And fill it with the grey light of a diamond.

The heart grows stronger and stronger

By shower of such abundant wealth.

We return to our home, holding our friends hand in hand.

We sleep in peace by trusting each other.

Only Love and Light Remains

Mighty of the mightiest may ever rule this world
With all their dangerous artilleries and weapons.
Fear broods in our hearts.
Aversion and distrust may barricade our soul
Within the thick wall of enmity.
But, like the light of a small flickering candle is enough
To brighten the spirit in any depth of darkness.
Like the first rays of morning light,
Always and ever defeat the darkest of the night.
It is in the hope of all weak and perished.
It is in the heart of all lost and broken.
Only love remains and hate dies.

With shrewdest of deception, the clever ones might
Plight and plunder the paradise of love and peace.
Destitution and barrenness may spread everywhere.
But, like the freshness and youth of the lotus
Rejuvenate and enlighten the muddy pond.
Like a glad bird that knows not the strength of the sky.
It is in the innocence of a new-born.

It is in the songs of many unheard poets.

Only love remains and hate dies.

Come what it may from the deadliest of destructions.

But, like a storm keeps within itself desire of peace.

Like the joy of waves over fathomless deep Oceans.

It is in the light of endless stars and sun.

It is at the edge of farthest oblivion.

Only love remains and hate dies.

Take Off

I sleep and woke up every day,

Eat and drink.

Sing and cry.

How do I ever know to what and where it goes?

I fly from branch to branch.

Travel from place to place.

With or without any purpose.

I wonder why this haste, why this ignorance?

The stubbornness of mountains

That never says what it has to say.

The rage of ocean waves that clamour loudly.

How do I ever know their hidden aspirations?

Through escalation, love, and light,

I feel this undefeated joy.

Through fathomless fall, sorrow and darkness,

I feel this victorious pain.

This unstoppable music that plays through me,
Play through all.
How do I listen to it and know its words?

The light of hope flutters its
Wings to reach the treasure trove.
The echo of heart whispers several names
Of a repository of peace in dreams.

Following such an unceasing spirit,
Let us go far from the aviary of our vision.
The true discovery is going beyond the horizon
Away from all the noise of the world,
Let us listen to the music of life in utter peace.
The true rhythm lies in following our hearts.

This invisible yet powerful cage of fear and doubt
Can only be broken by wings of free will.
Let's fly away from this emptiness,
Into a new beginning.
Into some new air.
And in that quest.
In that persistence of struggle.
Let us escape this living.
And escape this death.

When it Rains

The frogs croak and jump here and there,

The whistle of pouring begins.

Come out everyone.

Do not stay in your home today.

After a long summer of tortured heat,

The sky weeps and cries.

And after months of waiting,

It rains today.

Bursting of many beings around.

Mouse from their holes and ants from theirs.

People are running briskly to find shade.

Tyres of vehicles steer the road.

And splash water on legs everywhere.

Someone slips or falls somewhere.

Pouring can get heavy,

Do not hasten,

Wait somewhere,

When it rains today.

Leaves smile brightly in this musical bath.

Fish in the pond cheering and jumping from water to air.

The peacocks in the forest dance in their ecstasy,

Swaying their feathers around.

The beauty and strength have come to all

In this shower of love,

And everyone is totally wet

As it rains today.

Quest of Ages

Where are you?

See-through

Can you see, my dear heart?
That it is not mere beauty of a lotus,
It is the expression of a whole pond.
That it is not only form or perfection all around us,
It is the expression of a whole universe
In the creation of being.

Can you listen, my dear heart?
The subtle music that goes out in the world.
That it is not mere chirping of birds in the morning,
It is the song of the feast.
That it is not mere rustling of leaves,
But it is the joy of the unknown,
Immeasurable and unseen wind.

Can you be my dear heart?
In this fleeting ecstasy of life.
That this is not the mere unknown play of children,
It is bliss, pure joy and freedom from all the known.
That these are not mere songs of a poet,
It is true love, eternity beyond time.

The Mirror of Self

It's only you, my beloved friend,
Who throws many colours to colour me with your joy.
But it's only you who is always colour
With the colour of my love.

For you, all our triumph and disaster are one.
But it's only you who can make even our mere presence
Akin to any great victory.
In the wake of the night, you rob all our dreams.
But it's only you who shows us a dreamy world
In your dark and fathomlessly deep eyes.

With our separation,
In longing,
We wander beggarly.

But when we find you,
It's only you who give us a great wealth
Of your love and kisses.
And fill our heart with overflowing pleasure
And our words with no meaning.

Defiance

Today and now.

In low voice or loud.

Speak O' brave women.

Speak to the whole world.

All that is ever lost to you.

Whatever injustice done to you.

Speak eye to eye and face to face.

Speak O' rebellious women.

Speak to an unjust world.

Do not hide behind the veil of tears.

Do not wait further, for any right moment.

In the crowd and at your home.

Speak all about your glory

And in-numerous sacrifices done.

Speak O' glorious women.

Speak to the inglorious world.

What if they reject you?

What if they played you fool

With their deceitful promises?

You must ask what is rightfully yours.

You must ask it again and again.

Speak O' fearless women.

Speak to the dishonest world.

From your care and compassionate gazes,

You have sewn the pain of all whom you loved.

But from your questioning eyes,

You must break apart the wickedness

From this great world.

Speak O' daring women.

Speak to the ignoble world.

Hope of Clouds

White like cotton hanging deep in the sky.

When clouds cover the sky,

A solid roof form on our head, and being dispersed

They take innumerable shape.

Now, a wind from the Far East is here,

And suddenly moving everywhere.

Where did they go?

In hopes of rain.

In hopes of shade.

In the summer or winter.

Whenever we see them.

We ran towards them.

Clouds with no rain do not make our hopes weaken.

Only some little drizzle did not break our hearts.

What if they disappear?

We wait patiently for them to come again.

Somewhere far a glint of white light.

Somewhere deep our heart awakens.

Unrest builds up; our legs go running,

And brisk in pace.

To see where they go?

To catch wherever they go.

We all gather.

We all ran towards them.

This year was such heavy pouring,

This year happiness everywhere.

Yet, to wet in this rain again and again,

And to quench our eternal thirst.

In hopes of joy.

In hopes to fill our empty pitchers.

Whenever we see clouds in the sky.

We ran towards them.

Migratory Songs

There is a glint in your eyes,

Whenever you see us,

Whenever you shy.

There is a song in my heart.

And you know I am singing.

Don't take your eyes away from us.

Don't stray us from any worldly story.

A candle beside us flickers and dies.

And you know I am singing.

You whisper stories of the world,

But honestly, we don't care.

But you care for all our pain,

And that makes us so glad.

A gentle breeze that blows your hair.

The way you braid it.

With askance, the way you look at us.

And you know I am singing.

When you depart,

When you say good-bye.

But when you stop often

And return to say things that remain to be said.

When you leave not and wanted to stay.

Then you know I am singing.

In your loneliness.

While doing your daily works.

When you stop thinking about us.

And a fleeting smile comes from nowhere.

Then you know I am singing.

Last Drop

It is just one sip my friends,

That this heart always seeks and enquires.

And it is only one sip from him that is always withheld.

It is one sip that is a priceless drop of wine.

And it is only one sip of more pleasure.

It is one sip that is a glance of her eyes.

And it is only one sip of elixir of a whole life.

It is one sip for which an artist's thirst

Is fiercely running after.

And it is only one sip that is less perfection.

It is one sip for which this empty bowl of the

Heart remains forever thirsty.

And it only one sip that is dropping from the pen

Of a poet in his life hereafter.

My Seditious Heart

There is no rest, no sleep to him.

If I ever closed my eyes, I see lightning in them.

If I am all alone than I listen to thunder in my ear.

A big storm always kept hidden

Deep within my heart.

If it had swum across all the ocean

And found the priceless treasure,

There is no glory in him.

If it had drunk purest of the purest

Still there reside an unquenched thirst in him.

A big ocean always remains to be sailed

Deep within my heart.

Standing against all odds.

Ready to face the mightiest.

Ready to climb the highest.

Of many struggles fought and won

But there is no peace in him.

Many unreachable mountains

Are always remained to be conquered

Deep within my heart.

All are Drunk

In this great house of thirst,

All are drunk, lost and scattered

Everywhere in their drunkenness.

Everyone is taking a sip from this huge barrel

But without any cup or bottle.

All are drinking but not only with their mouth

But with their eyes and ears too.

Drinking for many years of their lives,

They have reached nirvana.

And from where nothing can bring them down.

Every newcomer would enter with their demand for taste

And though all are abundantly served,

Their thirst never gets completely quenched.

In their drunkenness where they are,

All are seeking a drink that is more refined,

More processed.

Whose taste is eternal and that cannot be

Found in common.

In this great house of thirst,

Lovers are drunk.

A Deer is drunk with the freshness of the forest.

Bees with the nectar of flowers.

Moths are drunk with rays of light.

Ants are drunk in some serious duties.

And birds.

Oh! Don't ask about them.

They are the master.

They are taking the best.

Purest of the purest.

Have you ever seen their eyes?

Their heads never still.

There is a story about them.

Everyone knows here.

Once they were earthly beings.

Living and walking on the ground with all others,

But someone gave their hand to them,

Pulled them on high altitude

And getting husk of what is best they lost themselves

And never came back to what they were.

From that day onwards,

Their aspirations lie only in the sky,

High and above.

Every flight they take only to get one sip of air

And quench their quenchless thirst for some moment.

Wonder why only they struggle to get their wings,

While no other dares to try

And still totally unaware of what precious

Thing lies above.

This is such a big house of thirst.

And all are drunk and mad with choices given.

All are drinking from air, water, light,

And music present around them.

You show us your collection,

A bottle filled with the different colour of the liquid.

But ours are different one;

Nothing can be matched with it.

You say your drink is fermented for many years.

But ours are kept from the start.

Now you are counting years on your finger.

You say your drink is classier or processed

With many flowers or fruits.

Oh! You are very new here,

You sway too much.

Imagine ever plant, every flower on earth

Giving their fragrance freely in the air.

Now your head is spinning.

You must sit somewhere, don't fall down.

Our drunkenness and our sobriety are one,

Which is very different from yours.

Do not give your drink to any of us as

This drunkenness will go away.

In this great house of thirst, all are drunk with a drink

That can bring life to the dead and

That is present everywhere.

You are so Lovely

Your lovely face shines within me

And brightens my whole day.

In your ambiance, I am like a candle,

Burning and melting within.

You hold my hand with such possession,

My heart flies like a kite in the wind of your love.

You smile whenever you see us,

And before we met,

My heart would be completely

Wet in your shower of gaze.

You sit beside us, and music starts to play somewhere.

You are smiling.

You don't believe us.

You say it is all made up or dreamy talk.

Bring all the holy books and I shall take a vow on them.

And still, if you do not believe us.

Then it's fine with us.

Our life, dreamy or real is incomplete in every world,

And you are a door to all of that.

We enter these many worlds inadvertently.

Our day-and-night drift towards "where are you."

From you to you.

To complete them.

But still, you are smiling.

You don't believe us.

But it's fine with us.

Craftsmanship

I will be still.

Nothing to move me from where I am.

Resolutely standing and facing

Everything coming in my way

I will not cry out a word when hammering will be done

On me through many hard adversities of my life.

When pointed chisel of daily small sacrifices would

Carve my beauty with the depth of delicacy,

Then with all courage

I will be standing still and be not moving.

I would never shy or take away my face

When joyful hidden mirth

And loud laughter within some great friendship

Would paint me with its deep embedded colour.

When music and songs will raise and tune my heart

And fill it with the harmonious rhythm of life

Then I will be listening in peace and be not moving.

When all crafting will be done then I will wait

Until a true artist would come

And give her finishing touches to all my statuary self.

With her spirit of love and care.

Her hands-on my hands will burst my veins

With the new vigour of blood.

When her still eyes would reflect

The beauty of my true being

And show a new world different from here

Then I will be still and only looking into her eyes.

At last, with all grace, when she will take my head

To her bosom to fill my chest with some eternal breathing

Then I will be completely surrendered

To her and be not moving.

Dawn of Sunset

My old friend.
Come out of your home.
Come out today.
Let us shake this hopeless world,
And make it upside down.

If your legs are tired and slow,
Then we will stop everyone who will go ahead of us
If the distance of the road seems more distant to you,
Hours take many hours to pass.
Then we will change all the goalposts very near to you.

My friend, come out from your hard-wired territory,
Where you have confined your primitive and crude self.
Come out of your prison.
Let us shake this dispirited world,
And make it upside down.

If all the colour of life seems colourless to you,
Then we will paint this whole world only

With the colour of your heart.

If the beauty and incense of the flower

Did not melt your statutory self,

Then we will pluck them all and

Lavishly spread on your way.

If music and dance did not create

Any rhythm in your heart,

Then we would call all artists and

Play your songs of the heart.

My friend,

Come out from your barren world of aversion.

Come in all season.

Come surely in a season of love.

Let us shake this joyless world,

And make it upside down.

If the mirror of your home pinches your grey hair

Or it may show the wrinkle on your face,

Then throw them outside and never buy them ever.

If youth and adventure pass beside

You with pace and smiles their wit,

Then you must smile wisely at them.

If you have won all the difficult crusade in your life

And sit with solitude in a corner of a deserted house,

Then come out from your castle of solace

And let us find a contest impossible for you to win.

My old friend,

Come out of your home.

Where you are deeply sunk.

Where you have made a thick wall

Of pride around yourself.

Come out of this graveyard.

Let us shake this passionless world,

And make it upside down.

The Discoverer

It is the most distant course that comes nearest to thyself, and that training is the most intricate
which leads to the utter simplicity of a tune.

– Gitanjali, Rabindranath Tagore

Spread it all through and over,

My severe pain and pangs of sorrow.

Let my eyes fill with sweat

And sour mysteries of the various seasons of life.

Destroy all my sure and absolute convictions.

The big hoaxes of heightened fear.

Let this life born again and again

In many new songs of strange love

And the wisdom of unknown lands.

Bring here through all directions.

Heavy storms with the wrath of lightning and thunder.

Let my restraining brim over

And spread its wings in many unrestrained moments.

Drown me in the ocean of burden.
Let my existence throb in painful struggles.

When clouds of hope held far in the sky
And my heart is groped in some sad music.
When the light of stars is rarely seen
In the darkness of gloom.

In this far oblivion.
At this land of solitude.
Let all my life's endeavour loses its meaning
To find it in the joy of mere presence.

Threshold

The turmoil of pain you feel

In your bones is not going to stop.

You must leave this dark place of doubt.

Rainy storm brings several implicit whispers in the ear.

Thunder in deep clouds chills your legs.

The vision of a shattered future

You see is your imagination.

Your fear is your imagination.

To get stuck in one place for so long is to die.

What is the weight of the leg that

You cannot lift it from yourself?

Whose entreating voice holds you from behind.

Stifling within the heart makes you ill.

Bear no duties, take no grudge.

The longest hours are hours of pain.

At this juncture, several ushered and amplified

Choices hover above your head.

In life, the music of drums and beats

Surrounds us everywhere.

Yet the music of life has pause in it.

You wonder why you keep coming

And rolling down at this adverse situation.

At this lowest ground.

Life on earth is a great circle,

Yet life on earth has gravity in it.

Let's start your journey a fresh.

Mustering all strength in only the next step ahead.

Taking only one step ahead.

These clouds are temporary.

These clouds will fade.

The Story of a Florist

A merchant boy in town sells flowers and smiles.

He lives on the outskirts of town,

And he always comes and goes from his home.

In winter or summer, rain or autumn,

Boy comes and goes all years.

With his tattered cloth and with his uncombed hair,

He roams everywhere in town.

To all passers-by, to all men and women,

To whomsoever he meets,

Wherever he meets, he greets them

With his fresh flowers and a pleasant smile.

His flowers are always fresh,

Collected only in the morning.

His flowers are of varied colours and kind,

Collected from many gardens.

But his smile is unique and with it,

He sells fresh and colourful flowers

Throughout all the years.

He never gets sad or depressed such

That his flowers may look droopy.

He never gets tired easily.

The fragrance and freshness in flowers

Keep him fresh too.

Boy sprinkles water upon his flower's day and night.

He blossoms with his flower's day and night.

The boy is energetic and quick;

He goes running door to door,

Street to street and sells his flower

With his smile day and night.

He looks at all young ones with many hopes.

He shows the redness of rose with many hopes.

In despair, sometimes he gently pleas

To people to buy his drooping flower.

But he doesn't ask too much money; he is so modest.

And he never asks anything for his smile.

The poor sod sells all his flowers with a smile.

The flowers sold by him go to many homes,

To many people and thus perfume of those flowers

Goes on spreading and spreading.

The lover buys his flower in hopes it may bring

A smile to the face of their beloved.

And perfume of love and smile

Goes on spreading and spreading.

But the boy doesn't know all that.

So ignorant and innocent he is.

He doesn't know what he sells and what he gets.

But whatever and how much he gets

He takes only with a smile

And sells his flower with all grace in his heart.

Sometimes he travels a long distance to some other town.

The travellers going with him buy his flower

Because he keeps them always fresh.

Those who are poor and wealthy,

All buy his flowers because his flowers are always fresh,

And the boy is wealthy too and

With his wealth of the smile,

He sells flowers wherever he goes.

The merchant boy scatters and propagates

The fragrance of flower and fragrance of his smile

Everywhere in town and to many people,

Whomsoever he meets and wherever he goes.

Our Play and Conversation

Is this the sea of your eyes?

Or I am drowned in the depth of some great pleasure.

Is the whole world is spinning around?

Or I am heavily drunk from the

Fleeting gaze of these two barrels.

These are one of your ways to

Enchant me with your magic,

Else how come our conversation lasted

For all night but felt only a moment.

You must have many tricks with you.

Otherwise how come I keep looking at you

And every other face disappears from memory.

You are speaking to my heart from subtle murmur,

Silent whispers, and songs of your anklets,

And I think it's raining without any clouds.

I would be glad to know the key of all these puzzles,

But you hide behind my heart to let me be puzzled.

I asked to tell us what our love is about,

Then you show me this endless sky.

If we are going to play these games, then I am lost forever.

But you show me otherworldly games,

And I am saved in the game of love.

Being curious I ask how to win these games.

You say to keep playing and losing.

Our conversation goes on like this.

Our life squandered day and night

On many such sweet useless plays.

And we live with no deduction,

Nor with some judgment and never

With any dignified ambition.

The Master Poet

What more special poem that I would give you here?
Which of these words will raise your
Heart and replenish it with delight?
You must leave this book.
Go out from your home today.
If you want to see and feel the real treasure from yourself,
Go to wherever your beloved friend is.

Where is she?

She is the master of phrases and expressions.
In meeting with her, hold back all your thoughts.
Let your heart do the talking.
With complete attention listen to
Everything unsaid by her.

When two souls are in love who will impart
Greater wisdom than that.
Which joy is ever so pure?
Many big secrets of the world can be

Learned by the wink of an eye,

By some subtle gesture than these many words here.

Come the next day enlightened

And getting the vessel of your heart completely filled.

Find any paper and pen beside you.

The adoration and humbleness with which you see

And feel the love of your beloved

Write anything that comes in your mind,

Until whatever that glow inside

You may appear before you.

The City of Love

Dust swirls around and the wind
Is aghast with grained stones.
The burdensome legs deranged and strayed far-

Ah! My Friend,
The wayfarer of lonely paths.
A bird of passage in a deserted land.

There is great jubilation goes on in the city of the heart.
The place is shimmering and scintillating with
The plentiful radiance of light.
Here, whoever is awake has reached to the treasure trove.
On this path to pathless land,
You chase the myriad of things which are far,
Gleaming and permanent.

But you lose that which is so near, urgent, immediate
And constantly changing, and therefore,
You forever remain lost.

People of this city are falling in love again and again

And dying to their forlorn self.

Here, resides the sea of abundant life,

Foaming with smiles and ripple of songs without

Any resistance to what is.

Joy lies in the spontaneity of actions,

Without any memory.

But you live inside time;

Therefore, you remain farthest and unconquered.

My friend,

The traveller of darkest of the night.

The seeker of love, light, truth, and beauty.

In this city of hearts, spring of youth showered daily

In the hall of eternal thirst.

From their lips and eyes,

We are filling the pitcher of bottomless hearts.

A gust of wind with immigrant incense

Brings the message of strangers beyond all borders.

The rhythm of our feast is trembling

And shaking the cosmos of the universe.

But you always close yourself to your senses,

Therefore, you remain outside this city.

Light your own lamp my friend-
As the way of this paradise is through treachery
And crookedness of gloomy shadow of thine own.
Dawn of enlightenment is squeezing its eyes
Through the fog of the patient heart.

And you must throw all your true discoveries and wisdom
Like children throwing pebbles in the ocean
And come to this portal of eternal peace of love,
Which is your true home
And only it is here, who you truly are.

I am Always Late

They always complain about me, whenever I reach home.
They ask the reason "why I am always late."
But how do I tell them what stories happened on the way.

When I started my journey in the early morning,
Mists in the air wet me completely.
And taking the bath of pure freshness
My pace was slowed and strayed.
While passing through the garden,
My eyes were hooked to the various
Colourful flowers in it.
Their enchanting fragrance kept me in the grip of
Drowsiness for many hours.

As the sun was scorching above the head,
The shadow of the big Pupil tree
And sweet voice of Cuckoo
From hidden branches clasped my tired legs.
All afternoon was squandered in listening to her songs
On the courtyard of their houses,

When the unknown play of some children
Filled the joy in the heart
Then there was no way to shy away from them.

At the sunset, drinking for many turns
From the golden pitcher of light
My evening was completely lost.
Anyhow, I scramble to reach the home in the late evening.
Standing at the gate they enquired into my whereabouts
And asked why I am always late.

I stood silent and never spoke a word.
Their wise words were all over me
But they never saw my gleaming
Eyes and peace on my forehead.
They did not smell the perfume that was all around me.
They were heedless of songs that were on my lips
And mirth of pleasure in my heart.
I stood silent and never spoke a word.

In the midnight, eluding all of them
I came at the rooftop to sleep under
The blanket of moonlight.
Finding my bed empty in the morning
They searched for me everywhere.

Kunwar Siddharth | 121

Soon they found me on the roof, sleeping peacefully.

They understood something in themselves

That why I am always late.

But they never saw the paradise of dreams I was held in.

You Shall be the Truth

You will be the truth.
Only be the truth.

You will always seek it and live with it.
You will not be afraid to speak about it.
You will not be afraid to listen to it.
You will always question it but never mould it.

You must protect it but do not seek any reward for it.
You must share and spread it,
Yet the truth is omnipresent.
You will carry it and hold it like a child
In your lap without any burden.
You've to believe in it with the depth of your heart
But do not make religious out of it.
You've to set it free like a bird from its cage.

Let it not be a pity that you endeavour
All your life but failed to get it.
Let it not be a pity that for the truth you
Stand no one stands with you.

Mighty hearts never bother what is win or loss.

They never sought such old prejudice.

A garden, full of flowers,

Nurtured by a true gardener since a hundred years before.

His work did not go in vain.

Fragrances of flowers ferment in the air

For such long years.

A cool breeze filled with unknown fragrance

Raises the heart of a wayfarer,

Who is lost in some lonely and strayed path.

With awakening eyes,

He searches and finds the true path

That leads to his destiny.

You will be the truth.

Only be the truth.

And shall ever be the truth.

The Crescent Moon

I followed every path to the small echo of your voice.
I ran after wherever you have cast your shadow.
In-depth of my songs, in awakened dreams,
Whatever I sought; I sought only for you.
I know not this light that takes me through
And shows me a way to the darkest of the night.

Like rays of the sun, after traveling long-distance
Reaches to the moon and reflect back to see it.
Let all my songs, all my useless wanderings
And many small efforts go only towards you,
With all their strength.
And what if you may or may not
Close your eyes or heart for them.

A moon that shines within me will come in the sky
For the whole world to see.
And in the light of these poems.
Let my love scatter and reach to the people
Beyond time and in all dimensions.

If you will ever call me,

I will come out from the graves of all my death.

The Unbroken Processions

There is a caravan of people going
Towards their love and aspirations.
All beings are moving ahead.
Every person's hand is held, and none left behind.
One who sleeps, one who runs, both are going.
Patch on the road, scattered bed in the morning,
Are proof of that.

One who goes for a long journey
In search of priceless treasure.
One who stays in his home for the love
Of comfort and peace.
Both have found and learn something
In their course of life.
Both have to tell stories about themselves or the world.
Either something happened to them,
Or they did something.
There is a caravan of people going towards love,
And all are taken with it.

The Solitary Triumph

My determination and raised heart

That spend over useless strife of no worth.

Everyday work and sweet painful struggle

That brought utmost happiness and peaceful sleep.

When I succeeded in doing something difficult,

But no one was around to clap.

These are my secret victories

And I keep them in my heart with all grace.

When my friend got my back for any mistake I did,

And they like me even more.

Those big risks that I took when I decided to do nothing

About something desperately asserted to do.

The courage of going nowhere and following none

When persuaded by pleasure

And plays that always go outside.

These are my secret joys

And I live them, fill my heart with much gladness.

My soft smiles and loud laughter that come daily

In many unnoticed and inattentive moments of life.

Those times when I stop often in my walk

To fill my vision with the beauty of the world around.

These are my larger moments

And I wear them as a garland of flowers around my neck.

Withheld

Lest, it will rain, you choose not to come under the sky.

Lest, it will be a shame,

You have missed the rhythm of the dance.

Lest, it will be the darkness, you choose not

To come in the light of stars.

Lest, it will be pain, you choose not

To play the game of love.

Lest, it will be the death, you have held far from life.

Let as all Return

Glorious days are over

And now we shall only be working and living.

Way till here,

Our days were filled with many ecstatic

Ventures of fantasies and delusions.

Now let us return to what is thirst, food, love, and play.

Our victory was big and clamorous.

We had known ourselves to the whole universe.

But now let us return to what is small and innocent.

Hands are too strong to hold a flower.

Be gentle, lest not a single petal may be lost.

Ages have gone by in the creation

Of these in-numerous flowers

And in-numerous being all around us.

Now let us all return to what is meant to be a flower

And what is meant to be a living being.

Refugee

Seeking you, this heart has lost

What was once dear to him.

Home, friends, self-respect, reason, success,

And everything that can be called sanity.

For one world another was gambled and both were lost.

Now, my heart finds momentary solace in music, poems,

The play of children, and the flight of birds.

Enigma of Death

Death, it is who my breath knows you well,
Therefore, it had never stopped running since birth.
Every moment of life it had to wrestle
Its way through and through
Until the next breathing.

Death, it is who my heart knows you well,
Therefore, breaking all shackles of prudence
It had stretched its arms for any impossible
Dreams and the strange love.
It had a dance over mere fleeting cadence
Of subtle music that spreads freely in the air.

Death, it is who my life knows you well,
Therefore, day by day it has blossomed
With colourful beauty around it
And open its buds to sunshine
And mist of pleasure and pain.
It has kept oneself unharmed and
Peaceful by living voluntarily
In the shade and the labyrinth of many illusions.

But it is death which mysteriously

Hides by a curtain of uncertainty,

Making each moment of life complete

And adventurous without any burden of time or fear.

A Voyage to Us

This boat is our home, my love.

Though it may be old, vintage and rusted.

Though it may be wrinkled by the

Waves of time and tides.

Come aboard to make it all new and

Decorate it with your passion

And let us go so far where no one can find us.

In the dim light of early dawn

When all morning birds may be asleep

In their warm and cozy nest.

When dewdrops have not touched the youth of lotus.

You come swiftly and stealthily without

Making your anklet sounds

And without your skirt touching the

Chords of rustling leaves.

Let us go so far so that there is no word,

No shame, and no rhythm for us.

It is only you and I my love to listen, play, sing, and dance.

Let us go so far so that squirrel and deer

Do not see us kissing at our love tryst,

Besides the bank of the river.

Sky does not peep through clouds,

Playing the game of shadow and light.

The light is you my love, shining and kissing

On the dark corner of my heart.

Let us go so far with this wind, with swift-flowing waves.

Let us go beyond the depth of our own ocean heart,

Where there is no shore, no country

To reach, and no pearl to find.

It is only you and I my love,

Finding and reaching to one another

On this great voyage to the shoreless sea of our love,

Where there is a perfect union.

Together

Life is a grand festival.

In this gathering, all have come carrying with them

Many bags of hopes and aspirations.

Dumbstruck by grandeur and beauty;

We walk hand in hand.

Exploring every street and shop in our way.

Every meeting is a new celebration.

For our merry-making, food and drink lie

Abundantly on the table before us.

The sweet that we share in this meeting

Give its juices to mouth in our bitter or painful moments.

Songs that we sang together are raising our

Hearts in every silent and lonely path.

A pearl of the chain knit together

By the thread of air we breathe.

A bouquet of colourful flowers,

Giving fragrance to each other.

Different notes of music, creating a symphony together.

Life is a long journey

From the youth of the fountain to the ocean of death.

We are a river flowing briskly in this passage of the world.

We are drinking from each other.

Those groups of birds that come and go

Through several places years after year.

Covering thousands of miles,

Crossing every border and nothing to hold them back.

They travel with wing to wing.

Sky to the sky.

Season after season.

Through dusty storm and in heavy rain.

Lest some may not lose their way or can get lost,

Those birds of passage fly together.

When Death comes and whispers to me,

'Your days are ended,'

Let me say to him, 'I have lived in love

And not in mere time.'

He will ask, 'Will your songs remain?'

I shall say, 'I know not, but this I know,

That often when I sang I found my eternity.'

– Rabindranath Tagore